WHAT I'M ON

Camino del Sol

A Latina and Latino Literary Series

WHAT I'M ON

LUIS HUMBERTO VALADEZ

The University of Arizona Press
Tucson

The University of Arizona Press
© 2009 Luis Humberto Valadez
All rights reserved

www.uapress.arizona.edu

Library of Congress Cataloging-in-Publication Data

Valadez, Luis Humberto, 1982-
   what i'm on / Luis Humberto Valadez.
     p. cm. — (Camino del sol)
   ISBN 978-0-8165-2740-3 (pbk. : alk. paper)
   I. Title.
PS3622.A38W47   2009
811'.6—dc22   2008037223

Publication of this book is made possible in part by the
proceeds of a permanent endowment created with the
assistance of a Challenge Grant from the National Endowment
for the Humanities, a federal agency.

Manufactured in the United States of America on acid-free,
archival-quality paper.

14   13   12   11   10   09   6   5   4   3   2   1

for Graciela Vigil
jefá

CONTENTS

WHAT I'M ON

dear reader: this is what i thought on easter day

this work wrestles with itself, despite the temptation to project tar.

I give you what I have to give.

Of utmost importance, the environment taught me that this work
didn't have to be a platform from which to extract revenge against my
existence.

search for the intention behind the initial sentiment.

illuminate the possibilities of existence to a young man who saw the
world as merely black, white, brown, and without redemption.

What is presented in these pages chronologically displays this young
person's progression of understanding.

present it despite fear of hindsight

rally against an inflated self-conscience looking for gratification in the
form of striking out against an audience.

This, I would learn, was not the case.

There was a time in my life when I believed that merely scraping off
the mildew of my visage and writing about what I saw underneath was
enough to emancipate myself from the unfortunate events that comprise
an existence that shaped my perception.

Getten Rid of Histree

Yain't no: gettin' slapped for hidin' mom's
cigarettes/ raped cuz ya yelled "run, girl, run" to
sum twelve-year-old wen you wuz six/ addicted to
weed at twelve/ shitty relationship with ya brothas'
fatha better den watt you gots wit yors havin'/ A. A.
momint at thirteen at ya ex-boy's ex-girl's house
havin'/ whupped for bein' up while moms was
drinkan'/ gettin' yor foot on fare in the allay/
jumped cuz everybodi gots ta git jumped/ three
brokan ankulls gettin'/ knowin' the shootas and the
shot/ feelin' bad for Santiago dyin' of hurt failure at
fourteen even if his brotha tried to kill ya/ wiren'
money home cuz sumwun stol his car got polled
ova ran and lef crack roc init and he need to git ta
impownd so he kin go ta work on mundane/
catholic mass den protestant sorvice goin' to/
lookin' threw ya self in the mirr jus to see the
pattorn of years of murmuring contempt to ya
image/ wishin' mom wuz dead cryen' at it and
beghen' ta sleep in her bed/ waitin' til college
gradiation to make love/ no love havin' to make/
GodbeautybeautyGod hopin' for/ groundloss fallin'
no hed held up by gravity/ nonsense no good starin'
figor/ young ghetto Latino poet new voice for
generation competition love me I'm oppressed hard
time lines under my eyes read my book poet

chiquito

chiquito was
cold tired and fearful
i wanted to take him home

i held him
first in my arms
then in
after his neck snapped

lord god
please take him to that
other place

he poked his head
through my prayers
and fell through the roof
you'll hold him better
than i

Taurus in the Sixth Cusp

I used to listen to a song about a man called to work.

And how it made his functions harder.

He couldn't articulate his need to relax.

And the weights on his legs forced him to scream.

I believed he screamed in a rather mediocre and enchanting way.

And the way his throat moved caused me to react.

About the potential that my life could reflect his past.

And I want to share this song with you, but.

I can't get the day off work.

Raymond

used to walk
        through the alley
                off the street
                        near the house
when we lived on 21st

six years old
      I observed him
I would do this at ten
when after wrestling practice
we'd shower
he'd stand naked   away from the team
proud of himself

at that time
      I didn't know him
just observed that
he walked past
my house each day
and when he got
                to a point
midway between
the train tracks
and my backyard
                  he'd start to run
toward Chicago Road

one day I thought
safely I could yell at him
little kid to big man
little man to little kid
I yelled
then hid

Kil-lahhh!

(after Harriett Mullen)

You are my inspiration beyond my Jesus
    my role model beyond my Julio Caesar Valadez
    my sexy emulation when you scream "Kil-lahhh!"
You are my "jackin' mugs all day" when my hood movie ends
    my vocabulary teacher beyond my Ms. Smart
You are my "don't mess wit dem foos on Main" beyond my religion
    my gov mint beyond my lawful breath
You are my lover through rape
    my rapist and personal trainer
    my "lift dat bar punk!" when I tear
You are my intimidation for the sake of lustful fear
    my Latin beyond my King
    my King beyond my Count
    my Gangster beyond my Disciple
    my Four Corner beyond my Hustla
    my Vice beyond my Lord
    my Eight beyond my Ball
    my Solid beyond my Four
You are my sleeping with the dog beyond my big target on my back for ridicule,
harassment, violent humiliation, death, lock-up, painful initiation, alcohol
erasing trauma, numerous children livin' in my momma's basement off what
little I make sellin'
You are my mother's concern beyond her eighty-hour work week
You are my role model beyond my Julio Caesar Valadez

Section 5

I put cream cheese on your bagel
then tomatoes

I gave it to
your disgusted look
your picking off slices with neat fingertips

you looked at me
the way i would stare at the person
who shot my dog

Could you put some more cream cheese on this?

i didn't say anything
to the green plastic plate
i passively thought to it while i spread

Nine years old:
José García
put a thirty-five to me
my mother was in the other room
He would have done us both
if not for the lust of my fear

Mars Sesquiquadrate Jupiter

You
make
me
expand
the
place
I
avoid
       in
       a
       project
       that
       involves
       that
       I
       decorate
a
room
I
had
never
dreamt
of
entering.

Talkin' Shit to Dharma

another phone call
the innocence-stealin' trucker
is in town
get questions answered
get money
if you can
see his looks
do you live up to his photo?
him and mom
drinkin' beer
she don't know
you're unborn
sister will show you hers
on a car ride
after showing her yours
she'll be surprised it wasn't the
downstairs people
surprisingly unaffected
she'll seem
mom don't know
sitting on Jose's and Julio's laps

Walking Home from the Bus

I suppose it's time to think about the phone call
Eight years old (home from a baseball game)
Do you like talking to me?
I guess

This is what I think about when it's cold or hot and I'm cold and hot
This is the charge needed to reciprocate the energy that motivates the movement that
puts a dent
inside your very small face

I walk away and wonder if
The chargeenergymovement (required of an athlete)
Is the same required of those who assault
I wonder if growing is painfully the same

From Behind the PACE Bus Station

I know that my father would hate me/ should hate me

I know that he curse my/ should curse my kin

I know that My Lord God
should be my protection/ would be my protection

My father/ my mother
My mother/ a slave
My brother/ saved
My brother/ the darkest
My sister/ my father

        I know that My Lord God should be my entourage
                      amongst tagged garages

        My bare face knows its mark/ a target

        I know that MyLordGod should be my protection
        But the man I seek looks like you

no cops/no parents/no memory

they jumped me
    collecting money for my paper route
gaby and his cousin who could not speak *inglaze*
    in the parking lot in front of school
I was coming from School Street
    where I never delivered without sun
I had a chance but I pulled up sagging pants
    got hit
    then kicked
    repeatedly

I thought about how I used to burn leaves
    not in a pile
    one at a time
    with a lighter
    sitting cross-legged

They jumped me
        We were on a downstate wrestling trip
Raymond and Milk were two of Chicago Heights'
        best

In the hotel room
        They drank with coaches all night
i got slammed against
        then hit
        thrust
        repeatedly

i thought about how tape heads can erase
        as soon as they record

versus

perhaps you think I don't know what I am talking about.

we are not the same so I can kill you, get it?

In the end there is a conflict between what you want and what you're
meant to be,

The upbringing laid out in these pages is fraught with the oscillations
apparent in any life, really, but they inevitably even out like any
sine wave.

What am i sposda to do?

dictate to y'all: love me, feel bad, feel guilt, I deserve something
for this pain.

I realized the role perception and visualization played in separating
those disparate grains of humanity that walk around from the dirt we
trample daily.

we ain't the same, so it ain't no thing to kill you, get it?

you are doomed to a life that ebbs and flows with the circumstances
surrounding it?

and let the practice, and My Lord God, do what it got to.

Capricorn on the Second Cusp

Slower,
I hold an offer
the same as any that feigns to dictate sorrow.

Longer,
I hold that whatpastmind
I do not want to increase.

You would be paid
what you are worth

but I have not gone
to heaven.

Neptune in the First House

musicians upon our dependencies

escaped to the long bed where

we released what we released

and we were mediums

colored

without familiar contact

tiresome conditions arise against

and don't let you notice quickly

that I'll lead you tonight

Jesus Sestina

Jesus was righteous
His only begotten son
made love to the sinners
made them dinners
some say he was a yogi
the bible cannot confirm he was not a vegetarian

can't form a what not
hit sweet
me who say
the blinding son
hems a dam in
a vet who rest

confronts the sinners
no con for get
met din
hit seas
on sent got no
we say so

yo mess was
dem have sit in
on be ghost see
i be cot for not vegan
jew right
with nourishing dinners

det here
the patience of a yogi
west
no mo svelte
ran ot o cant
let on

is lone oh shen
did he em die
turns them into vegetarians
mess wi he
sonnets
set swat to jeru

I forget the righteous like a set son
And see sinners have more dinner
And pray gangsters and yogis sit as vegetarians

eatin' wit' Christ

i want to do those things/ the things we talk about over the
radio/

i was thinking about the broken glass from the basement
window/
and prayed that you'd bless the wood that broke it/

i want to speak in generalities like they are my children: only
I understand them/

i can't figure out how to make my analogies make sense/

You remember when i was a ned flanders born again christian/
people would say "wotsup" and i'd be like "I gots
Jesus"/ you knew back then i couldn't stay at elim
pentecostal or st. agnes/ too many jewish friends or maybe
not enough fear/

although I did fear when they talked about you/ i remember
a dread-locked preacher on t.v. once/ screaming about how
everyone even christians got it wrong and how they are
going to hell/ he pounded his pulpit as a signal for the boy
on his right to read another passage/

he made you sound most scary/ then i went to sleep/

when i woke up/ i missed you/ for about a week until the
doctor gave me pills that made me act like i didn't care/ i
still tried to find you though/ but you was never home/ at
least not at my house/

eatin' wit' Christ

the constant drones are feeding loud people/

the genial man next door boarded up the window for
free/ i couldn't find a decent piece of wood or nails/

the way that poets understand but don't pander so i
can talk to canines/

i'm asking what to say/

i wanted without a past but i couldn't without walking
through these narratives/ even the "little christs" got it
wrong/ my chest pounded as the pastor stirred my
fear

he liked to scare belief people and belief in people
and belief into people/ he liked to tell four books'
scary stories/ his sermons deformed beliefs/ i called
him for help/ he told me i was a sinner/

wit' Christ

You give me a collect phone call/ i can accept his
charges but not his guilt/ i don't want to father a
grown man

how do i keep this brother, Christ?
locked in a room?
away from beings?
sentient or not, an open wound is infected when
airborne

what do You do, Christ?
when prayers are heartfelt the way a surgeon
operates?

Christ as Bastard

even Your pops
took off
when things got hard
                according to the book

even You were prodded
with sharp sticks
You didn't want
                inside

does that mean
that i might
perhaps
be closer to
like You
than i thought?

Because i'd like that

Section 18

there's an altar in the house
        veneer oak dresser

a cloth draped over
        artificially aged lumber

a four-foot crucifix
        pained Christ

a rosary hanging from His neck
        Christ pained

candlesglasssaints and gabriel
        AZTEC GOD ASSIMILATED

john paul II in a frame
        leftover from Polish tenants
michelangelo's pietá
        a glass reproduction

a picture of the harvest Virgin
        holding a prince son
        miniature her
        like an extension of her appendage

Section 13

I get son
righteous write sonnets
sinners beg the sea

 I get debt there
righteous won't forget
sinners cannot confirm

 I rent love
righteous send swats to Jerusalem
sinners let Him die

 I can't be gettin' to ask Him the questions
with righteous confessin' sinnas gessin' for dem
what is my go to me?

potato peeling

I like them because I have memories of peeling potatoes for my mother so she could cook them with eggs, chorizo, or red sauce for the family;

I like potatoes because my family had no money and potatoes were cheap and filled us up easily;

I like potatoes because I woke up to them when my mother, who worked every minute she could, wiped time to make breakfast on Sunday;

I like potatoes because they were there when there was absolutely nothing in house.

Even in saying these things, there is much more to my declaration on potatoes.

So how do I peel away at these layers the way I used to peel the potatoes?

frontin'

i anagram and look and subject to deformation and reconfiguring

For example:

I saw past love/ and wasn't happy/
I saw past love/ and was lustful

becomes

Esau past love/ san wand/ vast awe/ lul

it ain't events or blocks that ahm jettisoning through this process

it be layers of meaning, identity, narrative, and ego that gets peeled off

i can only increase my own understanding

So who is my audience?

whatever there is for anyone else is their own

Section 7

gangsters and yogis and vegetarians
    cannot confirm
    they can't form a whatnot
    a vet ran rest

gangsters and yogis and vegetarians
    are not the lone ocean
    won't mess with sonnets
    can't rent love

gangsters and yogis and vegetarians
    forget the righteous like a set son
    hit sweetly and make sure
    no con forgets

And my subjective "eye" versus this collective "we"
    messes wit he
    sees debt to hit
    is a beggar who
    rants what he can't
    and asks
    "did He let 'em die
    to let my go to me?"

Mercury in the Second House

You were pressed to react,
permit a new avenue
overlooking a field
with radio towers.

I used to teach
how to keep what you speak,
but as I gain signal strength
I can't keep from
signing the contract
that would redevelop
your property.

Gemini in the Seventh Cusp

The song I wrote about sharing with you is still restless in my head.
I think that when I leave I'll want to sing it to you.
I think that I'll want to sing it to you today.
And I know soon I'll be singing it to you in a different time zone.
Please forgive me; I want to contort you the only way I know how.

radio

list ad/ makes you/ self what
en akes/ possi/ wor change/ urse
don veto hat/ sor at it
feels/ air less/ blade need be
at akes hir round rip/ sel bade/ mote
with place/ where more/ radio alone
a feed tri limp/ til ant be let/ faath
cing wit less
pit very/ get lace/ lit heed
can vile/ see the dai son/ hil rey nel
reyn on
vile can
very lace
les faath
be let
mote feed
akes
change
wor
veto
rip

if you listen to the radio
it makes you feel impossible
as if you were the challenge to yourself
you don't have to like what it says or what it does

or what it feels
none of that makes the air around you less crisp
less of a blade
or promotes less of a need to triumph over impossibility
you still want to be a bullet
unfathomably piercing the air
spiting everything in its place
until you die where you can't live anymore
because the radio is on while you're alone

esau past love

i saw past love
        Esau passed love
and wasn't happy
        san wand
i saw passed love
        Esau past love
and was lustful
        lul

caring eyes run rotting
        Esau past love
rig constructor's matrix
        he saw passed love

my matrix is thinking
        about your matrix
and how your matrix
        perceives my matrix

neurosis is a doorway
        me saw passed love
but not to no where good
        me saw past lust

don't understand we other

you goddamn bastard
want to touch my sister

mad must tar

mood start

stand

gard man gon'

doom

must dust

to toy

dad

mister mutt come

tan hot mane

resist mist

name her

star to ant

resist stomach

such term

nun

wrist now odor
dart hot bust
such wane

is ache wet
rats sit in tot
dog sit in man
doom mister

stand

the won category

slur/ bastard/ slur
won category and
bloodshed/ matrix

a storm on an audience
wet clothes/ unsatisfied
a storm on an audience
again

a storm on an audience
wet clothes/ unsatisfied
a storm on an audience
and soon you'll make me feel good
the norm of an audience
apologize/ slur
a storm on a confidence
not similar
slur/ bastard/ slur
now i've won your category and
bloodshed/ matrix

i'd like to be you but i'm busy with me
can i get your designated contact
i'd like to be you but i'm busy with me
combination of letters and numbers?
i'd like to be you but i'm busy with me
i think i'll feel better once i buy something
i'd like to be you but i'm busy with me

are you a storm on an audience?

Dharma Talkin' Shit

Get rid of the history
and rage won't
be your sexuality

Get rid of the history
and realize the blurred line
between phallus and brain

The desert fathers said the prayer of the heart for twenty or thirty years

Lord Jesus, have mercy on us
The trick was to say it with their heartnotface

copulate power
not in lording
but in a place to stand
not in elating fear
but in holding a mutual stance

Get rid of the history
and back acne won't put
hearts tears

Get rid of the history and
walk through your narrative

Moon Semisquare Uranus

find myself brave

being conductive

passed like infatuation

erratic without cause

boredom will pass

the things that align my spine

Moon Conjunction Moon

I
did
not
enter you
to make your plans.
Just
to
climb
your stairs.

Saturn in the Ninth House

In the way that maturity
combines with stroke
to cause death
and delayed seclusion
feels like duty
less connection resides
and in being adult
we fancy ourselves
instructors
intact and honest
we enter the city
because it approaches

Taurus in the Sixth Cusp

I used to listen to a song about a man called to work.

And how it made him function harder.

He couldn't articulate his need to relax.

And the weights of his log forced him to scream.

I believed he screamed in a rather mediocre and enchanting way.

And the way his throat moved caused me to react

over the potential that my life could reflect his past.

And I want to share this song with you, but

I can't get the day off work.

Moon Square Venus

rather during darling
dominate am too
ends more push
than opposite
pose social permit
can set back
eyes fragrance love

Sun Semisquared Uranus

In return
for an eye
to the direction
not of travel
or return
but toward
your period
of grace
I'll take
the abrupt incline
toward the face
of belligerence
and avoid that
which produces
other ties.

Stabbed in the Neck

Luis Valadez (29) died on July 11, 2012, hours before his thirtieth birthday, in what at press time investigators are ruling a homicide. He was shot seven times in the back and then stabbed once in the neck while painting over the LKN tags on his seventy-one-year-old mother's garage.

According to a note found on his person, he had just returned to his mother's home in Chicago Heights after "realiz[ing] that the world they made is for them and that the hope they instilled in [him] must have served to make [his] inevitable disillusionment and decline sufficient enough for [him] to lose [his] capacity for moral understanding." The note continues, "They must have wanted me to walk into that new mall on 29th Street or one of the incense and bullshit shops or one of the stupid-ass burrito places on the hill and unload on some motherfuckers. This would be widely reported in the media as illegal immigrant violence or the act of a violent criminal from an unsavory background and geography. Inevitably, this would propel legislation to further encapsulate and isolate their world from our likes for anything more than labor." These statements, along with some allusions to what detective Rich Vega referred to as "sexual trauma that the victim may have experienced," and some apologies to friends and family members, are all that is being disclosed by the Chicago Heights Police Department at this moment. The presence of this note has led some to suspect that Valadez's murder was in fact an act of suicide, but Vega pointed out, "It's impossible to shoot yourself in the back once let alone seven times, but we will investigate the possibility that the victim may have stabbed himself in the neck."

He leaves behind a thirteen-year-old dog, Jake; two turtles, one of which was his namesake; siblings René, Ponch, and Elsa; and his mother and estranged father (who should not be reached for comment).

Yo Dharma

if the natural state of being
is to experience
all people's pain

and the enlightened
take this on
while the unenlightened
personally take

and if Christ fits into
this narrative somehow
even if
Pastor Pacheco says not

and if it takes a thousand lives
to realize this state
and ten thousand more
to practice within it
before reaching the neutrality
necessary to go home

is my neighborhood full of beings
with nine thousand
nine hundred
ninety-nine
left

if there's a me to fuk wit'

but then i thought to myself
　this sounds like someone who thinks
he's got something
　like a shirt or a coat or a dog
　or a name or hair or
　　a scar on an arm from jumping out of a moving
car or a cold or mostly clear mucous
　　or a heritage that conjures memories of calling
mucous mocos or a fondness for potatoes or a
job serving food to self-serving hungry ghosts who
can't fathom starvation or enough mental caulk to
fill the holes in a brief expelling history
　　or the expectation to write another good poem
　or a good poem or flatbread or pickles or an
　upbringing that neither embraced flatbread nor
pickles or a thanksgiving prayer to say in front of a
mother's illegal boyfriend or a chair with four ball
wheels three intact and one cracked or language
or a language or a clean box or memories of perms
and box haircuts or a challenge of impossibility or
snapped neck
　　　or a god crisis complex conflict or jars of
pennies or a reason to save jars of pennies
　or something to do besides write or writing
　or earth or plot or a name or ringing in the ears
　　or dead ossicles

ACKNOWLEDGMENTS

Luis H. Valadez would like to thank and acknowledge:

Graciela Vigil, for being a source of strength and inspiration; Francisco Nuñez, Renè Nuñez, Elsa Vigil, Jake, Lucky, and Luis, because of and in spite of what bonds us.

Bobby Popolla and the Popollas, for their hospitality and friendship; Erica Buttron, Margaret Loretta White, John Bert Stanton, Nick Lutton, Derek John Boczkowski, Sarah Willis, Erin Hellweg, Kim Sommario, Tameka Hemmons, Lynne Marie Meyer, William Mims (Q Storm), Greg Sato, Stirling Myles, Scott Wilkinson, Jesse Detweiler, Lawrence Armstrong, and Jennifer Emily Kirkpatrick, for their insight, support, and friendship.

Tim Z. Hernandez, Dayanna Sevilla, and their tribe, as well as Jason F. MacDonald and Doris Vargas, for being positive examples above all else; and Kate Ann Heidelbach, because of and in spite of what has bonded us.

Anne Waldman, Sonia Sanchez, Amiri Baraka, Samantha Wall, Thurston Moore, Junior Burke, Lisa Birman, Corina Lesser, Christian Moody, Indira Ganesan, Andrew Schelling, Reed Bye, Akilah Oliver, Elizabeth Robinson, Ringu Tulku Rinpoche, Jack Collom, Arielle Greenberg, Laura Mullen, David Trinidad, Tony Trigilio, Kerri Sonnenberg, Amina Cane, Karen Volkman, Paul Hoover, Maxine Chernoff, Rebecca Brown, Harryette Mullen, Mort Castle, George Wetzel, Maya Shewnarain, the staff of *Bombay Gin*'s issue 32, Naropa Café, and the Naropa Audio Archive, for the various capacities in which y'all have taught and nurtured me.

Chicago Heights, Illinois, and even the bad memories—from the kids who jumped me for my paper route money and forgot to take it, to the bastards that raped me, to all the friends who've put up with my shit: it's all in here somewhere.

Some of these poems have appeared in *Bombay Gin, Sliding Uteri, 26 Magazine, Summer Stock, Transmission, Asphalt, Slipstream, Columbia Poetry Review, Antennae, Tendril, ANIMES, 63 Channels, Symposium Magazine, The Lunch Book, and Wet: A Journal of Proper Bathing,* and in the online journals *dogmatika.com, Retort Magazine,* and *Watching the Wheels: A Blackbird.*

ABOUT THE AUTHOR

Born and raised in Chicago Heights, Illinois, Luis H. Valadez writes to compassionately erupt his experience and perspective on an unaware public as well as to empathize with a populace who, like himself, thought it impossible to identify with anything. He received his B.A. from Columbia College, Chicago, and his M.F.A. from the Jack Kerouac School of Disembodied Poetics at Naropa University. He is the recipient of the Lily Endowment and other awards from Hispanic Scholarship Fund. His work has appeared in esteemed journals such as *Columbia Poetry Review, Bombay Gin,* and *Wet: A Journal of Proper Bathing.* As a poet, musician, and performer he has shared the stage with Anne Waldman, Thurston Moore, Saul Williams, Jello Biafra, Strangers Die Everyday, and Against Me. He is currently a Program and Education Coordinator for Chicago HOPES. He lives in Chicago Heights.